Tractors

Contents

Tractors

Tractors help farmers to do different jobs.

mirror
windscreen wiper
steps

Lifting

This tractor has a spike.
It can lift hay.

JOHN DEERE
726

Pushing

This tractor has a bucket.
It can push soil.

661

Carrying

This tractor has a trailer.
It can carry hay.

trailer

Digging

This tractor has a plough.
It can dig the soil.

JOHN DEERE
9420

Rolling

This tractor has a land roller.
It can roll the soil flat.

land roller
4260

Pulling

This tractor can even pull a tanker!

JOHN DEERE
8120

Index